NEPHI, NEPHI,

The Scriptures Are True!

My children, my children, the scriptures are true!
I'm grateful to read them daily with you.
–Anita Wells

To Shane, who was like unto the heroes
of the Book of Mormon.
–Neal Anderson

Text © 2004 Anita Wells

Illustrations © Neal Anderson

Visit us at deseretbook.com

Library of Congress Cataloging-in-Publication Data

Wells, Anita.
  Nephi, Nephi, the Scriptures are true / Anita Wells ; illustrated by Neal Anderson.
    p. cm.
  ISBN 1-59038-307-9 (hardbound : alk. paper)
  1. Book of Mormon—Juvenile literature. I. Anderson, Neal. II. Title.

BX8627.A2W48 2004
289.3'22—dc22

2004005873

Printed in China   18961
R. R. Donnelly and Sons, Shenzhen, China

10 9   8   7   6   5   4   3   2   1

NEPHI, NEPHI,
The Scriptures Are True!

Written by Anita Wells • Illustrated by Neal Anderson

DESERET
BOOK

SALT LAKE CITY, UTAH

Nephi, Nephi,
the scriptures are true!
Tell me what they
say about you.

I followed the Lord
through desert sand
and sailed a ship to
the promised land.

Enos, Enos,
the scriptures are true!
Tell me what they
say about you.

I prayed all night
and I prayed all day.
Faith in Christ
swept my sins away.

Benjamin, Benjamin,
the scriptures are true!
Tell me what they
say about you.

I spoke from a tower
so my people could hear
that the time of the Savior
was drawing near.

Abinadi, Abinadi,
the scriptures are true!
Tell me what they
say about you.

I thought my message
had been of no use,
but Alma the Elder
heeded the truth.

Alma the Younger,
the scriptures are true!
Tell me what they
say about you.

Because I was wicked
my father prayed.
An angel came, and
I changed my ways.

Abish, Abish,
the scriptures are true!
Tell me what they
say about you.

Converted by my
father's dream,
I lifted and helped
my beloved queen.

Captain Moroni,
the scriptures are true!
Tell me what they
say about you.

I led my people.
We fought to be free.
I waved the title
of liberty.

Helaman, Helaman,
the scriptures are true!
Tell me what they
say about you.

My valiant boys
were brave and true.
Their mothers taught
them what to do.

Samuel, Samuel,
the scriptures are true!
Tell me what they
say about you.

I witnessed of Jesus
from high on the wall.
Arrows and stones
could not make me fall.

Brother of Jared,
the scriptures are true!
Tell me what they
say about you.

Our barges would be
dark in the sea below,
so I asked the Lord
to make sixteen stones glow.

Mormon, Mormon,
the scriptures are true!
Tell me what they
say about you.

I wrote our story
and kept the plates.
I died near Cumorah's
battle place.

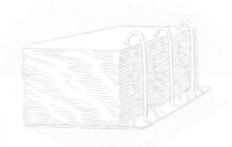

Moroni, Moroni,
the scriptures are true!
Tell me what they
say about you.

I was the last
of the Nephite seers.
I wandered alone
for many years.

Heavenly Father,
the scriptures are true!
Tell me what they
say about you.

I love you, my child,
I watch you with care.
How happy I am when
you seek me in prayer.

So keep the commandments
and do what is right.
The scriptures will help you
to walk in the light.

All the Book of Mormon
prophets testified of
JESUS CHRIST.
He is our Savior,
the Son of the living God.

And we talk of Christ, we rejoice in Christ, we preach of Christ, we prophesy of Christ, and we write according to our prophecies, that our children may know to what source they may look for a remission of their sins.

2 NEPHI 25:26